Bread Around the World

People all over the world eat breads of many kinds. The different breads are made from a variety of types of cereal grains (wheat, oats, buckwheat, rye, etc.) and come in many shapes and sizes. The type of bread produced by a cultural group is dictated by the environment which affects the type of grains that can be grown. The amount of interaction with other groups will also affect what types of bread are eaten. In many places where many different cultural groups live in close proximity, people eat a wider variety of types of bread.

Using the information pages in this unit:

The pages listed below have a small loaf of bread in the corner. These pages contain information about the history of bread, how grains grow, the process of making flour and bread, and the nutritional value of bread. These pages will need to be read to or with your students before discussing the information they contain.

Some or all of these pages can be reproduced for students to use in creating a bread information book of their own. The pages can be placed in a folder or kept in a portfolio with other activities until the unit is complete. Then staple the pages together in a construction paper cover.

Page 10 - *Bread is Good for You*
Page 14 - *Where Does Flour Come From*
Pages 16 and 17 - *Breads from Many Lands*
Page 18 and 20 - *The History of Bread*

Preparation for a unit on bread:

1. Check your audiovisual catalog to see what films or videos are available for you to share with your class.

2. Do some research to see who in your community can speak to your class about:
   - raising wheat
   - baking bread
   - ethnic breads

3. Determine field trips your students can take:
   - wheat farm
   - bakery or bread factory
   - mill
   - specialty bakeries

4. Speak to your school and public librarians and collect as many books as you can to use in setting up an information center in class. The bibliography on the inside front cover contains a few resources you might use, but is by no means a complete listing of what is available.

Bread Chant

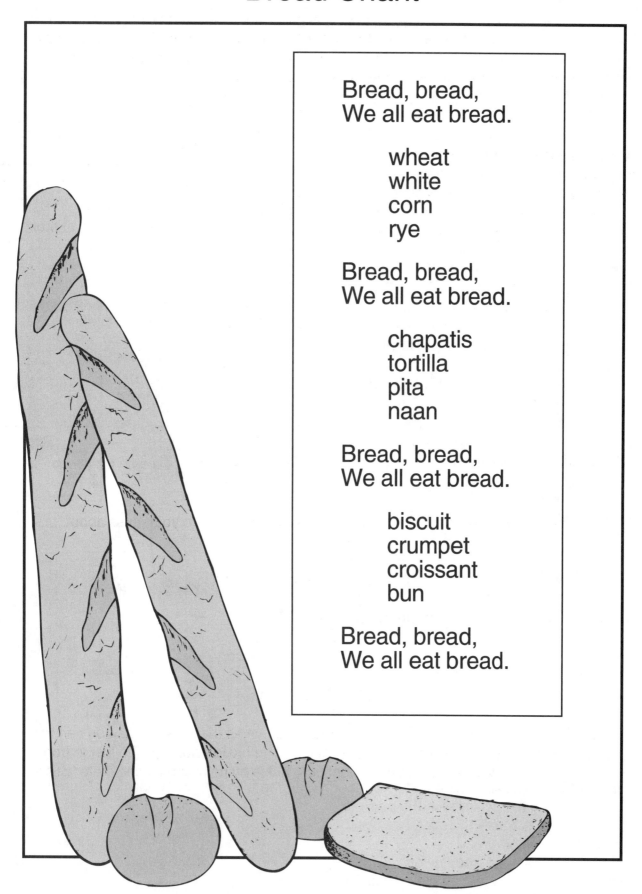

Bread, bread,
We all eat bread.

wheat
white
corn
rye

Bread, bread,
We all eat bread.

chapatis
tortilla
pita
naan

Bread, bread,
We all eat bread.

biscuit
crumpet
croissant
bun

Bread, bread,
We all eat bread.

Bread Around the World

Room Environment

Set up a bulletin board and learning center based
on the material you will be covering in this unit.

Bulletin Board

Cover a large bulletin board with colored butcher paper. Divide the area into two
sections.

Title one section **"Read the Wrapper."**
Pin empty bread wrappers and cracker boxes to this section. Be sure to have some
placed so children can see the nutritional information.

Title the other section **"Bread."** Put pictures of different types of bread labeled with their
names in this section. Use pictures from magazines, package wrappers, or pictures you
draw. These two sections will provide information for students as they do the activities
on the center table.

Attach manila envelopes as pockets to hold activity cards and work sheets. Write the
directions for each activity on the outside of the envelope.

Activity #1 - Have children make a list of the
names of the bread and crackers they see on the
wrappers and boxes on the bulletin board.
Challenge students to put the names in
alphabetical order.

Activity #2 - Put copies of the form on page 11 in
the envelope. Students are to fill in the blanks
using information off the wrappers.

Activity #3 - Put picture cards and name cards in
the envelope. (These should be copies of the same
pictures and words you have on the bulletin board.)
The student matches each picture with its name.

Activity #4 - Have children choose their favorite
type of bread among those shown on the board.
They are to draw it and write one or more
sentences explaining why that is their favorite.

Center

Place a table in front of the bulletin board. Provide the following materials for children to
use as they do the activities in the pockets.

- books about bread
- paper, pencils, and crayons
- an empty box for completed activities

Bread Around the World

Getting Started

Introduce the unit on breads around the world by having a brainstorming session. Ask questions such as these:

"What kinds of bread have you eaten?"

a. List these on a chart. Add to the chart as children remember other kinds of breads they have eaten and as you sample new types in the classroom.

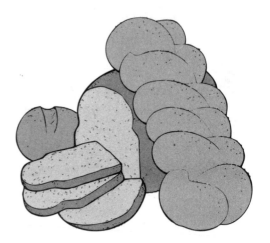

b. Use the list to categorize breads by types (raised bread, flatbread, crackers, etc.), forms (loaf, roll, bun, etc.), or grain/cereal from which they are made (wheat, rye, corn, etc.) as the unit progresses.

"Does anyone you know bake their own bread?"
"Have you ever helped bake bread?"

This discussion will help you determine how much your students know about the process of turning flour into bread in any of its forms. It will also give you clues to which parents to call to demonstrate some aspect of the bread-making process.

"What kinds of bread did you eat yesterday?"

List what the students ate at different times during the day. Have them explain the form in which they ate it.

---

breakfast - toast, biscuit, hot cakes, waffle, bagel

lunch - sandwich, pizza, hamburger or hot dog buns, burrito

dinner - roll, flatbread, bread pudding

snack - peanut butter and jelly on bread, pretzel, crackers and cheese

---

"What would it be like if there were no kinds of bread at all?"

Discuss what children would have instead of toast. How could they make a "breadless" sandwich? What would they do without hamburger buns and pizza crust? Encourage imaginative answers.

Have children illustrate one of their solutions and describe how it would be made.

"People all around the world eat bread."

"Look at these pictures carefully as I read the book to see some of these people and what they eat."

Share **Bread, Bread, Bread** by Ann Morris and Ken Heyman (Lothrop, Lee & Shepard Books, 1989) with your students. Use the photographs of bread and people enjoying bread to begin a discussion of breads eaten around the world.

List the types of bread shown in the story and the country in which it is being eaten. Help your students locate these countries on a world map.

"Let's keep track of all of the breads we eat for the next week."

Pass out copies of the form on page 8. Explain to children that they are to write down (or get an adult to help them) each kind of bread they eat at breakfast, lunch, dinner, and for snacks for the week.

My Bread Record

	Breakfast	Lunch	Dinner	Snacks
Saturday				
Sunday				
Monday				
Tuesday				
Wednesday				
Thursday				
Friday				

©1995 by Evan-Moor Corp.   8   Bread Around the World

 # My Bread Record

	Breakfast	Lunch	Dinner	Snacks
Saturday				
Sunday				
Monday				
Tuesday				
Wednesday				
Thursday				
Friday				

Note: Save the wrappings and boxes from the breads and crackers used in this activity to use on the bulletin board described on page 11.

Tasting Day

	like ☺	don't like ☹
bagel	ЖЖ I	II
pumpernickel	III	ЖЖ II
tortilla		
crumpet		
wheat bread		

Getting Ready
Bring in as wide a variety of types of bread as you can find at a local supermarket, bakery, ethnic market. Include leavened and unleavened breads, plus crackers, pretzels, etc.

You will need paper plates, a knife for cutting breads into "tasting" sizes, napkins, and plastic glasses for milk, juice, or water to drink as taste

Directions
Begin by showing each type of bread and asking, "Can anyone tell what this is named?" "Has anyone ever tasted it?"

Discuss what kind of flour it is made from.

Have children find the sample on their plate and taste it. Allow for very small tastes for your less adventurous students.

Provide time for conversation about what they are tasting as children finish all the items on their plates.

Do You Like It? Yes or No
Hold up each type of bread you have sampled and have children raise their hands to respond to the statements "I like it" or "I don't like it." Record the responses on the chalkboard, then ask questions such as:

"Which kind did the most people like?"
"Which one did the smallest number of people like?"

Bread is Good for You

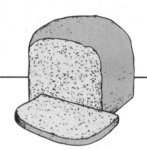

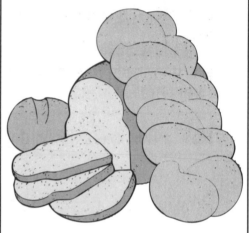

Bread, cereal, rice, and pasta are all grains or made from grains. When we eat these foods, we get many of the vitamins, minerals, and the fiber we need to be healthy, plus the energy to work, play, and grow.

Bread gives us many of the things we need to be healthy and strong.

- Carbohydrates and fat give our bodies the energy to work well.

- Minerals such as iron help keep our blood healthy.

- Calcium gives us strong bones and teeth.

- Vitamin B helps us digest our food.

- Fiber helps keep our digestive systems working properly.

Note: Use this activity with children who can read or send it home as a parent/child activity. Each child will need a bread wrapper to find the answers to the questions.

Reading Bread Wrappers

We can learn about how healthy a product such as bread, crackers, or cereal is by reading the wrapper or box. Look at your bread wrapper and find this information.

What is the name of the bread? _____

How much does the loaf weigh? _____

How much is a serving? _____

How many servings are in a loaf? _____

Find this nutrition information: _____

    Calories in a serving _____

    Fat in a serving _____

List the first five ingredients. _____

_____

_____

Cooking Demonstrations and Field Trips

Visiting Cooks

Invite people in to demonstrate bread making. Try to include a variety of bread types from as many cultural groups as possible in your area. Begin with the parents and grandparents of your own students. In addition to the knowledge these people can bring your class, it is a great opportunity to build self-esteem and to do some positive public relations. You may also have a professional baker in your community who would be willing to come and demonstrate baking an interesting form of bread.

Field Trips

Not many of us have a bread factory close at hand for our students to visit; however, we can usually find a bakery willing to let children visit. This might be a traditional bakery creating loaves of bread, cookies, cakes, etc. Or you might be fortunate enough to have a bagel bakery, tortilla factory, etc., nearby.

When going on a field trip do preplanning with your students. Discuss what they are to look for and what questions need to be asked. When you return from the trip, have a "debriefing" of what they learned. See if they can answer all of the questions developed before the trip. This is also a good time to write "thank-you" notes and/or pictures while everyone is still excited about the trip.

How Is Flour Made?

Bring in samples of as many of the following items as you can to show students as you share the information on page 14 about where flour comes from.

Types of flour and meal:
- whole wheat
- white flour
- corn meal/masa harina
- rye flour

Seeds: *(Try a feed store or health food store)*
- wheat
- oats
- millet
- rye
- buckwheat
- barley

If you live in a farming area you may be able to get actual plants to bring to class.

You will also need something with which to grind the seeds. Any of the following items will work.
- mortar and pestle
- old-fashioned coffee grinder
- flour mill (check with your bread-making friends)

1. Help children read the information on page 14. Let them see and feel the types of flour and meal you brought to class.

2. Use whatever grinding device you have and allow each child a chance to grind some seeds into "flour." Talk about how difficult it was for people to grind much flour before there were machines to help.

3. Use the cards on page 15 to discuss the differences among the various types of grains. Explain that the seeds shown on the cards are the most common ones used around the world, but in some areas other types may be used to a lesser extent.

Where Does Flour Come From?

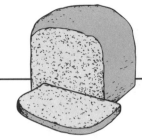

The flour used to make bread comes from the seeds of certain kinds of grass plants. Many different kinds of seeds are used. Each kind is ground until it is in tiny little bits. Long, long ago the seeds were ground using a heavy rock. Today we have large machines to do the work.

Some types of seeds are ground finer than others.

- White flour is very soft and smooth.

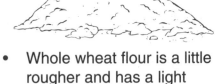

- Whole wheat flour is a little rougher and has a light brown color.

- Corn meal is yellow and very coarse.

- Flour made from rye seeds is very dark.

Each kind of flour makes a different type of bread. They each look different and taste different.

Rye

Rye grows in places where it is too cold to grow wheat. It can even grow in poor soil. Rye is used to make pumpernickel bread.

Wheat

Wheat grows in warm, dry climates. Wheat is used to make white and whole wheat flour.

Corn

Corn is a vegetable that can be dried and ground into a kind of meal. The meal can be used to make cornbread or tortillas.

Barley

Barley grows in warm areas around the world. Barley flour has been used to make bread since ancient times.

Oats

Oats are used to feed livestock and to make cereals. Some times it is added to flour to make oatcakes.

Millet grasses

Millet grasses can grow in all kinds of climates. In many countries millet is made into flour to use in bread and cakes.

Breads from Many Lands

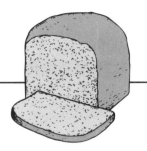

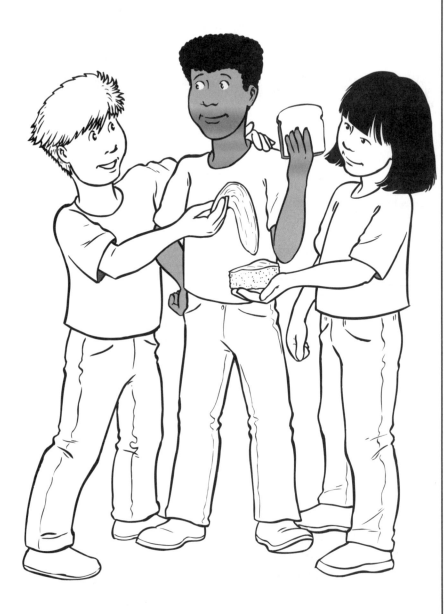

Each of the breads listed below were developed in a certain part of the world, but most of them are available for us to eat today where we live. How many of these types of bread have you eaten?

Flatbreads from the Middle East

Naan or *Chapatis* from India

Millet Cakes from Asia and Africa

Soda Bread from Ireland

Inferra from Ethiopia

Cornbread from North and South America

Tortillas from Mexico and Latin America

Different countries and cultures have developed various kinds of bread. As people have moved around the world, the breads they make have traveled with them. In places where people from many cultures live together, you find many kinds of bread to eat.

Bread in Celebrations

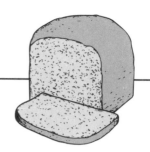

Jewish people eat a flat bread called matzo during the celebration of Passover.

Christians eat a kind of flat bread when they take communion.

In Scotland people eat a large, round bread called bannock on May Day to celebrate the arrival of spring.

People in Mexico bake special bread to eat at the celebration called El Dia de Los Muertos or "The Day of the Dead."

People eat a lot of bread as a part of everyday life. People also eat special breads for holidays, celebrations, and as part of some religious ceremonies.

What kinds of special breads does your family eat? When do you eat these breads?

The History of Bread

It took a long time for people to learn how to make bread.

In ancient times, people hunted for wild animals and gathered plants to eat. Men hunted for meat. Women and children hunted for roots, berries, and other plants to eat.

While they were gathering other plants, they may have found wild grass with ripe seed kernels. Outside the kernels were hard and bitter, but when they were chewed the inside would have tasted good.

People learned to grind the kernels between two rocks to get to the soft inside. This made a kind of flour. They also learned to add water to the flour. This made a kind of dough. At some time, people learned to cook the dough. This was a kind of bread.

At some time in history, people learned that they could plant seeds to grow more. The hunters and gatherers were becoming farmers.

Thousands of years ago, the ancient Egyptians discovered yeast. The bakers were able to make raised dough. Before this, breads were round, flat cakes that didn't taste like the breads we are used to. The bread the Egyptians baked with yeast was more like the bread we eat today.

The ancient Greeks and Romans were skilled bread makers. They made bread with finer flours and used yeast to make good breads. These breads were sold in public bakeries.

Bread was the main food for everyone in the Middle Ages. The rich lords and ladies ate bread made of white wheat flour. The poor peasants ate coarse black bread made from rye, oats, or barley.

Early sailors had to have food that would last a long time. The ships carried salt beef and pork, dried peas and beans, and ship's biscuits or hardtack. These biscuits were big, hard crackers. They lasted a long time.

Families used to grind their own flour. This took a long time for large families. The invention of the rotary mill meant a lot of flour could be ground in less time. These first mills were built by streams so that they could utilize water as the power source to turn the wheel.

Modern flour mills grind the kernels, but also have cleaners, sifters, and rollers to prepare finer flour. Today we can buy many kinds of flour if we want to bake our own bread. We can buy bread of all kinds in bakeries and grocery stores.

Wheat Seed to Bread

Introduce a discussion of the process of growing wheat to make a loaf of bread by reading your favorite version of **The Little Red Hen** to the class. Discuss the process followed by the hen as she grew her wheat, ground the flour and baked her bread.

Give children copies of the picture cards on pages 22 and 23. They are to cut the cards apart and lay them in the correct sequence on a sheet of large construction paper. Encourage children to have a neighbor check the order of their pictures before they are glued down.

The same pictures can be used to make a book called **From Seed to Bread**. Each picture is glued to a sheet of paper. The student writes one or two sentences about what is happening in the picture. The pages are put together in order inside a construction paper cover.

Planting Seeds

Get wheat seeds at a feed store. Have students help you plant the seeds in a large planter box or rubber garbage can. Place the container in a sunny spot. Water as needed. Place a notebook near the planter. Assign one child per day to observe what has happened and record it in word or picture form in the notebook.

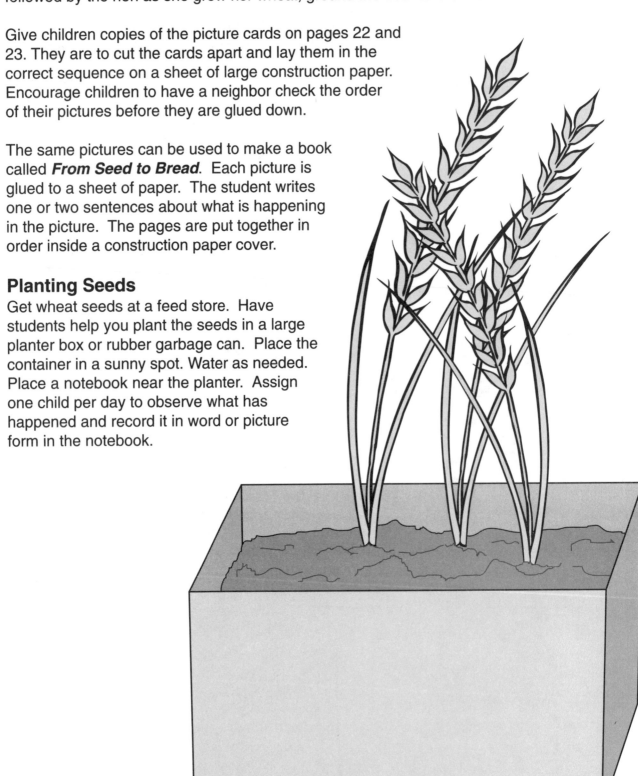

Planting Log

_____
date

_____
date

_____
date

Bread Around the World

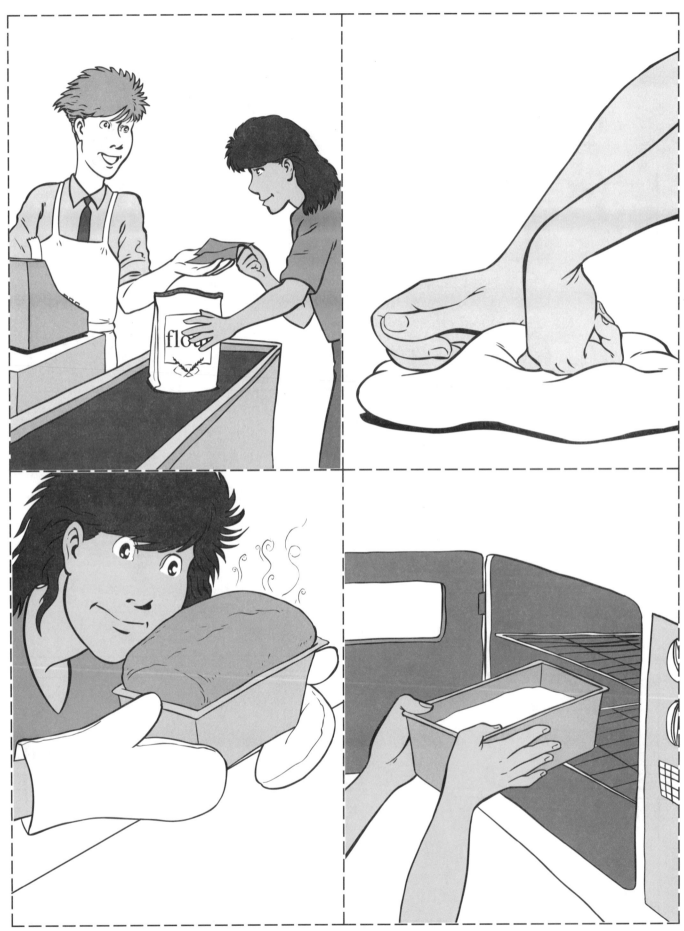

22

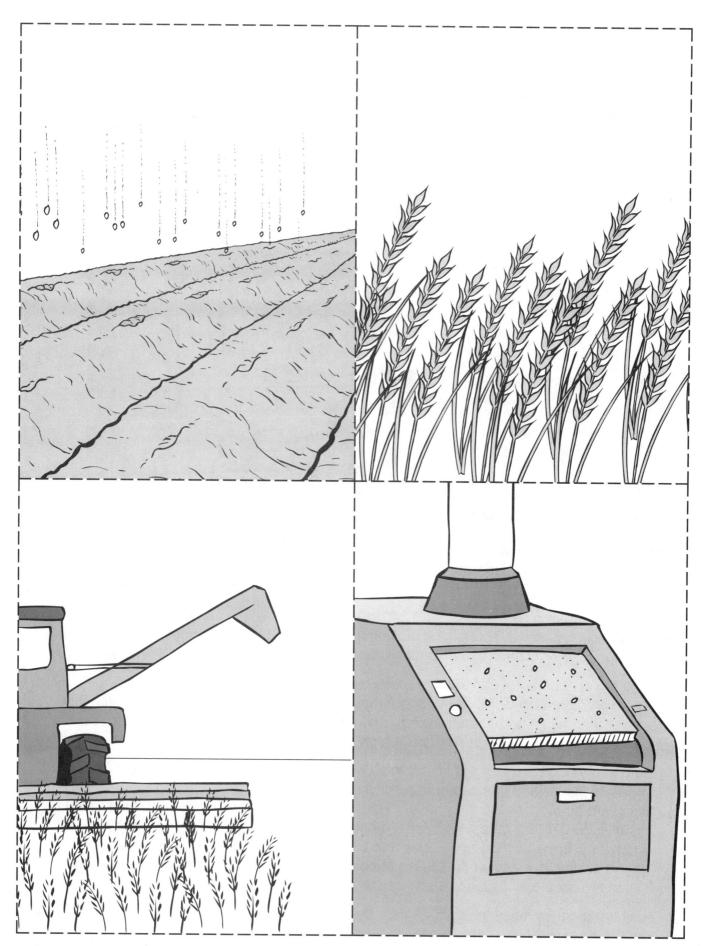

How a Bread Factory Works

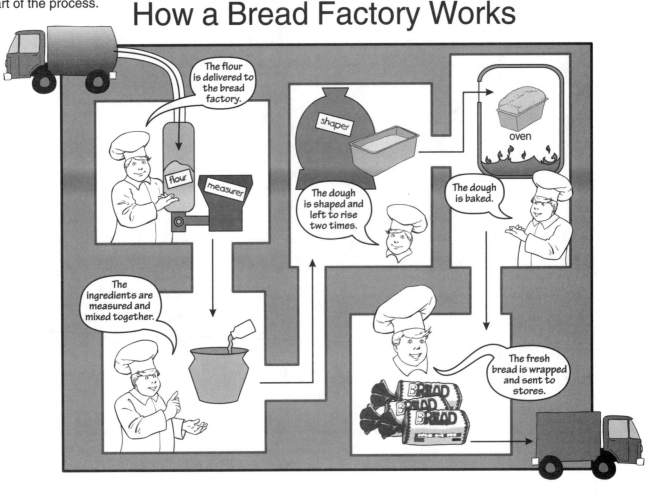

Factories have large storage bins to keep all of the different ingredients. The ingredients are moved to the mixing room where flour is sifted and put into a mixing "hopper." Then water and yeast are added. The mixture is stirred by revolving steel bars like a giant mixer.

The dough, called the "sponge," is put into a greased "vat." The sponge "rests" while the yeast goes to work making the sponge "rise."

Next the sponge is put into another mixer where more flour and the rest of the ingredients are added. Honey or sugar may be added. Salt, shortening, and vitamins are put in. Then it is kneaded (mixed) again and put into another greased vat to rest one more time. The dough will rise up high as it rests.

When the dough is ready it is started on a ride through the machinery. The dough is cut into even pieces and dropped onto a conveyer belt. The dough is shaped into little balls which are put on a belt to the proofer. Here the dough rests and rises until it is twice as big as it started. The dough is squeezed between rollers until it looks like a pancake. It is rolled up like jellyrolls and dropped into baking pans. The dough will now rest one last time. A moving belt carries the loaves through an oven. After being baked, the hot loaves are cooled and sliced, then wrapped and sealed.

Now the bread is ready to go on delivery trucks to be taken to stores where we buy the bread for our toast and sandwiches.

 Bread Around the World

Experiment with Yeast

Discussion

Ask "Have you ever seen anyone bake a loaf of bread? What makes the bread rise up high and fluffy?" If no one is familiar with yeast, mention that it is one of the ingredients in bread. Explain what yeast is to the extent your children can understand. List the answers given by children on the chalkboard. Explain that they will be experimenting to see which ingredients work to make bread rise.

Experiment -" *Looking for Gas Bubbles*"

Materials:

- one pack of dry yeast per experiment
- flour
- sugar
- warm (not hot) water
- clear containers of the same size (one per experiment)
- spoons (one per experiment)

Directions:

1. Set up containers and label them. Use nine parts water to one part dry ingredients.

   a. mix flour and water
   b. mix yeast and water
   c. mix sugar and water

   d. mix flour, sugar, and water
   e. mix sugar, yeast, and water
   f. mix flour, yeast, and water

2. Call up children to help pour and stir ingredients.

3. Leave the containers to sit undisturbed. It will take about two hours for the mixtures to begin to change. Have children take turns checking to see what is happening. They should see bubbles forming in the mixtures with yeast. The mixture of yeast and sugar should show the most change. Discuss what worked best and what didn't work at all.

Extension - *"Which Dough Rises?"*

Make two batches of pizza or bread dough with your students. Omit the yeast in one of the batches. Label the bowls "Yeast" and "No Yeast." Cover the bowls and sit them in a warm place for an hour. Check to see what has happened to the dough. Discuss what caused one batch of dough to rise and the other to stay the same size.

How does yeast work?

Yeast is composed of microscopic members of the fungus family. In a warm liquid such as bread dough, yeast grows and reproduces. As yeast digests the starch, it gives off carbon dioxide gas. The bubbles of gas get trapped in the dough. (Dough contains a tangled net of protein called gluten which has an elastic quality so it can hold the expanding gas.) The gas pockets expand, causing the dough to rise. The yeast in the bread dies in the heat of the oven, so no more carbon dioxide gas is made.

     Bread Around the World

Tony's Bread

Read *Tony's Bread* to your class.

Recall details from the story.
> What was Tony's dream?
> What did his daughter Serafina want?
> What did Angelo want?
> How did the three sisters help Angelo and Serafina?
> Why did Tony become sad when he visited Milano?
> What new kind of bread did Tony invent?

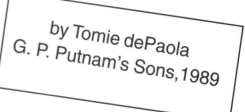

by Tomie dePaola
G. P. Putnam's Sons, 1989

Find Italy, then Milano on a world map.

Bake panettone with your class.

Getting Ready

1. Decide how much help will be needed. Ask for parent volunteers or cross-grade tutors to help if you do this as a small group activity. Ask parents to help provide the ingredients.

2. Write the recipe ingredients on a large chart.

3. If you make one recipe with the whole class, invite children up to help in measurement and mixing. If small groups each make a recipe, follow these steps:
   a. Give the supervisor of each group a copy of the recipe. Clarify how they will work with the students in their group. This is especially important if you are using cross-grade tutors.
   b. Set up a work area for each group. Have all necessary equipment and ingredients at the work area.
   c. Divide the class into groups.

4. Plan where you will bake the panettone (school cafeteria, toaster oven, send with parent to nearby home, etc.).

Cooking

1. Discuss what the measurements mean. Show the equipment needed to make the recipe. Explain each step.

2. Send each group and its supervisor to their work area with a copy of the recipe.

3. Allow ample time for mixing and rising. Children will have time to do other class work at various times during the process.

4. As each group finishes, label its coffee can or flower pot. Send the loaves to be baked, then have a milk and panettone party. Reread *Tony's Bread* as everyone enjoys the results of their baking experience.

Note: This recipe is based on one loaf only. Double the recipe if you are making it with the whole class.

Panettone

Ingredients *(for each group)*

sponge:
- 1/2 cup warm water (105-115 degrees)
- 1 package active dry yeast
- 1/2 cup flour

topping:
- 1/4 cup shredded almonds
- 1/8 cup sugar

bread:
- 1/4 cup butter
- 1/4 cup honey or sugar
- 1 egg
- 1/2 teaspoon salt
- 1 teaspoon grated lemon rind (grate for students)
- 1 3/4 cup sifted flour
- 1/8 cup raisins
- 1/8 cup chopped candied fruit

Utensils
- mixing bowl
- mixing spoon
- measuring spoons
- measuring cups
- pastry brush
- flour sifter
- clean cloth (for covering bread as it rises)
- waxed paper (sift flour on waxed paper)
- one pound coffee can or clay flower pot

Steps

1. Combine warm water and dry yeast. Let stand for 3 to 5 minutes. Sift and stir 1/2 cup flour into the yeast/water mixture. Cover and let rise about 30 minutes in a warm place.

2. Beat 1/4 cup butter until it is soft. Add 1/4 cup honey or sugar and blend until light and creamy. Beat in one egg. Add salt and lemon rind. Beat in the sponge from step one.

3. Sift and beat in 1 3/4 cup flour. Beat the dough for 5 minutes, then add the raisins and candied fruit.

4. Cover the bowl with a cloth and let the dough rise about 2 hours or until almost doubled in bulk. Punch the dough down and place it in a greased coffee can or flower pot. Brush the top with melted butter. Sprinkle the top with the shredded almonds and remaining sugar. Bake in an oven preheated to 350 degrees F for about 1/2 hour. Cool. Eat!

Make Me a Peanut Butter Sandwich and a glass of milk

by Ken Robbins
Scholastic Inc., 1992

Read *Make Me a Peanut Butter Sandwich*

Read the book to your class. In addition to explaining how wheat goes from seeds in the field to a finished loaf of bread, this book explains how peanuts are grown and processed into peanut butter and how milk gets from a cow to the milk container.

Make Peanut Butter and Jelly Sandwiches

Materials:

- peanut butter
- sliced bread
- small paper plates
- jelly
- plastic knives
- milk or juice and plastic cups (optional)

Steps:

1. Have children practice giving directions as you make a sandwich. Place a jar of peanut butter, a jar of jelly, a knife, and a loaf of sliced bread on a table. Have your students tell you how to make your sandwich. Do exactly what they say, no matter how silly. Let them correct their directions as you go along. Be prepared for a noisy, but exciting learning experience.

2. Set up working stations. Have no more than four children at each station. They are to share the ingredients as they make their own sandwiches.

3. Have children write how they made their sandwich (see form on page 29). Encourage them to write the process in the correct order.

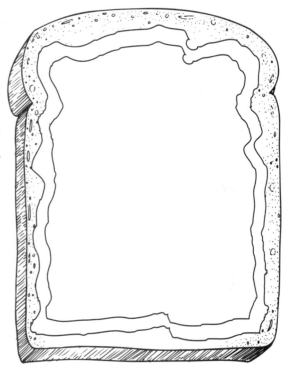

Or reproduce page 30 for sequencing practice. Read through the sentences with your students. Have them cut the sentences apart and glue them in order on a sandwich-shaped piece of paper.

Peanut Butter - Jelly

Teach your students the words and movements to *"Peanut Butter, Peanut Butter, Jelly, Jelly."* (See page 31).

Bread Around the World

Note: Use this form with the writing activity on page 28.

How to Make a Peanut Butter and Jelly Sandwich

First ____________________

____

Then ____________________

____

Next ____________________

____

Last of all ____________________

____

Note: Reproduce this page to use with the sequencing activity on page 28. Children will also need a blank sheet of paper.

How to Make a Peanut Butter and Jelly Sandwich

Open the jar of peanut butter and spread some on the other slice of bread.

Put the slice of jelly bread and the slice of peanut butter bread together. Eat it up!

Get out the bread, peanut butter, jelly, and a knife.

Now clean up your mess and go out to play.

Open the loaf of bread and get out two slices.

Open the jar and put a lot of jelly on one slice of bread.

Bread Around the World

Peanut Butter - Jelly

Peanut butter, peanut butter, jelly, jelly
Peanut butter, peanut butter, jelly, jelly

First you take the nuts and you grind them, grind them.
First you take the nuts and you grind them, grind them.

Peanut butter, peanut butter, jelly, jelly
Peanut butter, peanut butter, jelly, jelly

Next you take the grapes and you squish them, squish them.
Next you take the grapes and you squish them, squish them.

Peanut butter, peanut butter, jelly, jelly
Peanut butter, peanut butter, jelly, jelly

Then you take the bread and you slice it, slice it.
Then you take the bread and you slice it, slice it.

Peanut butter, peanut butter, jelly, jelly
Peanut butter, peanut butter, jelly, jelly

Next you take the knife and you spread it, spread it.
Next you take the knife and you spread it, spread it.

Peanut butter, peanut butter, jelly, jelly
Peanut butter, peanut butter, jelly, jelly

Now you take your mouth and you chew it, chew it.
Now you take your mouth and you chew it, chew it.

Peanut butter, peanut butter, jelly, jelly
Peanut butter, peanut butter, jelly, jelly

DON'T YOU TALK WITH YOUR MOUTH FULL!

Math Activities

Counting and Estimation

1. Estimate the number of slices in a loaf of sliced bread. Open the wrapping and count to see how close the estimates were. Repeat the activity with at least two other loaves of bread (of the same weight) to see if all loaves have the same number of slices.

2. Challenge students to figure out how many slices of bread you would need to make one sandwich for each child, and any adults, in class. When everyone has decided on their answer call on someone to explain how he/she found the answer. Then ask, "Did anyone find the answer in a different way?" Continue asking the same question until all methods have been shared with the class.

The activity can be extended by asking children to decide how many loaves of bread (based on the information from the preceding activity) would be needed to make those sandwiches.

Geometric Shapes

Collect a variety of shapes of bread slices (regular sliced bread, pumpernickel, pita bread, bagels, etc. - cut some slices into triangles) and flatbread and crackers (rectangular, square, triangles, hexagonal, and round). Take large sheets of construction paper (one per group). Draw and label a rectangle, square, circle, etc., on each. Divide the class into groups of four. Give each group either a bag of assorted breads or assorted crackers. Have them sort the items by shapes, placing each type on the correct space on their construction paper form.

Extend the activity by having children arrange the pieces into "bread people" or "cracker people." After they complete their pictures, have them draw a picture of what they have made. When the drawing is done, have them write the name of each shape they used by that shape on their drawing.

Patterning

Use the bread forms on pages 40 and 41 to practice patterning. Make a set of the patterns from felt or put Velcro dots on the back of each one. Use these to build patterns on a flannel board. Reproduce copies of the forms for children to use to copy the pattern you make, to continue a pattern you start, and to create patterns of their own. You can turn this into a center activity by making pattern cards for children to copy.

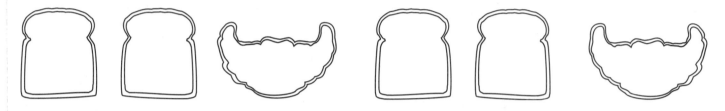

Word Problems

Make up problems involving amounts or costs of bread. This can be done at whatever level your students have reached. Write the problem on the chalkboard (using pictures if you need to), read through the problem with your students, then give them time to solve the problem. When they are done, ask for a volunteer to give the answer and explain how the answer was reached. Ask if anyone has a different way to find the answer. Share all the ways the problem can successfully be solved.

"I have to make sandwiches for five people. A sandwich takes two slices of bread. How many slices do I need?"

count
by
twos

$2 + 2 + 2 + 2 + 2 = 10$

Exactly the Same - Symmetry

   a. Explain that some things can be cut in half and both sides will be exactly the same (symmetrical). Show a whole slice of bread, cut it in half, and show the two pieces to your students. Have a child come up to lay the pieces on top of each other to show they are the same. Take the same shape of bread and cut it across the middle. Have children lay the pieces together to see if they are the same. Repeat this with several shapes of bread and crackers.

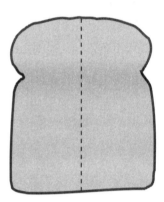 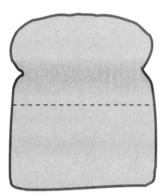

   b. Reproduce page 35. Have children mark the shapes at the top of the page they think are symmetrical. Then have them cut out the shapes at the bottom of the page and fold them in half to see if they are symmetrical.

   c. Have children find magazine pictures of symmetrical objects to share with the class. Have them look around the classroom for real objects they think are symmetrical.

Measurement

1. Children will be exploring measurement in cooking as they do the baking experiences recommended in this unit.

2. Children will practice either nonstandard or standard measurement using the "loaf of French bread" on page 36. Have children work in pairs. Record the heights on a chart or bar graph.

   a. Have children still at the non-standard measurement level use the loaf pattern to measure their height in "loaves."

   b. Have children ready for standard measurements use either the inch markings or centimeter markings to measure their height.

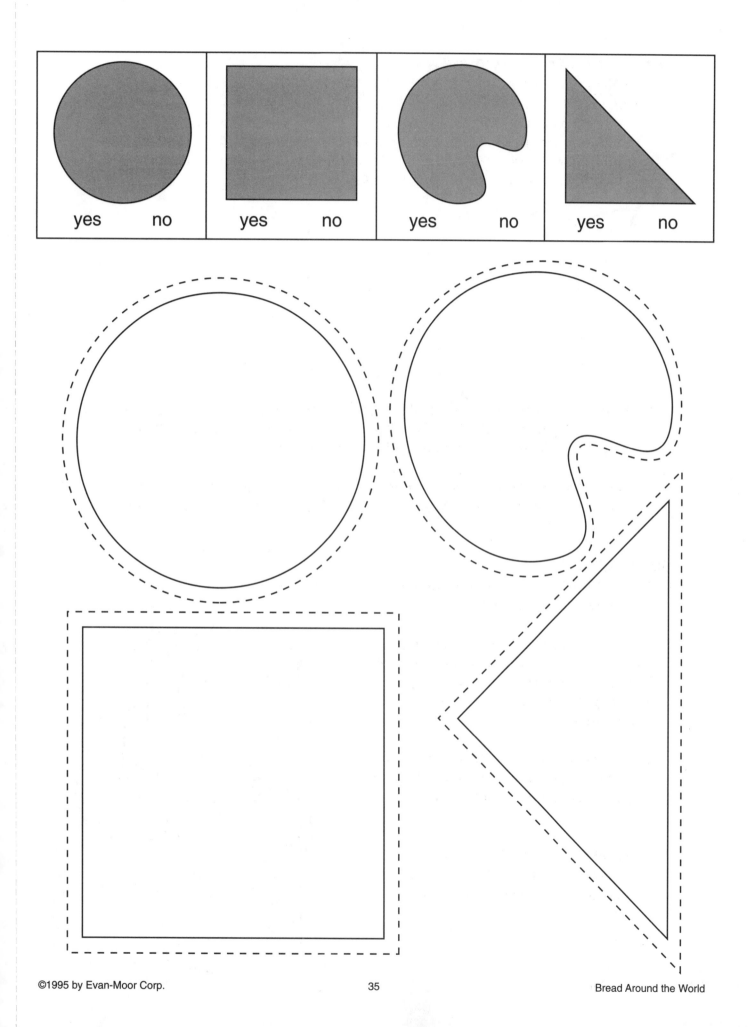

| yes no | yes no | yes no | yes no |

Measuring Loaf

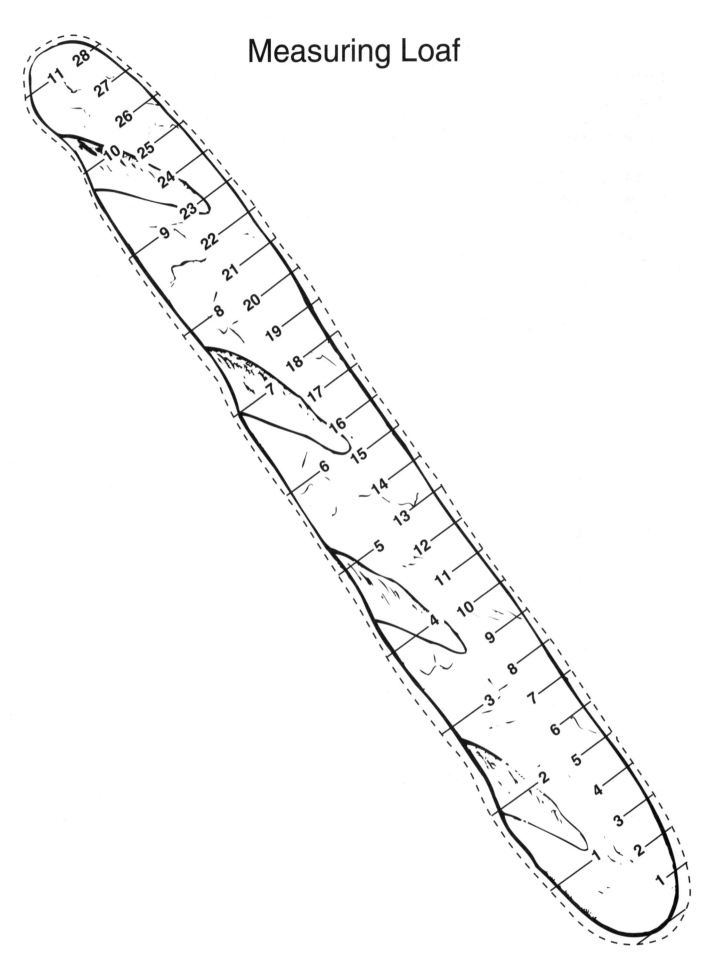

Bread Around the World

Language Activities

Phonics

You will be able to find words relating to bread for just about any sound you wish to work on with your students, whether it is simple beginning sounds (bun, biscuit) or the more complicated skill of recognizing blends (bread, crumpet).

Vocabulary Development

Use words relating to growing of cereal grains, making of bread, and types of bread to build vocabulary skills. Place the words you select on sentence strips for students ready to read them.

1. Descriptive Language

crusty	soft	hard	long
round	dark	light	tasty
heavy	sweet	salty	

2. Names of Grains/Seeds

wheat	rye	oats	corn
millet	buckwheat		

3. Types of Breads

loaf	wheat	rye	white
flat	pita	tortilla	cornbread
bread	bagel	roll	pocket bread
bun	biscuit	cracker	pumpernickel
crumpet	croissant		

4. Names for Parts of Bread

slice	heel	crust	loaf

5. Baking Terms

mix	knead	dough	rise
sponge	flour	slice	bake
ingredients			

crusty

tasty

tortilla

pita

biscuit

rice

dough

What is in My Bread Box?

Bring in a real bread box if you have one. Otherwise, use a shoe box labeled "Bread Box." Place a type of bread (real or a picture) in the box. Explain to children that you are going to describe what you have in the bread box. They are to listen carefully to your clues, then guess. After modeling the activity a few times, have children take turns deciding what to put in the box and describing it to the class. Give clues by size, shape, color, texture, and use.

"It is round and chewy.
It has a hole in the middle.
It tastes good with cream cheese." (bagel)

What's in my bread box?

Alphabetical Order

Use the vocabulary your students are learning about bread to practice alphabetical order. Use the bread forms on pages 40 and 41.

1. Reproduce enough pages of shapes to have 26 loaves of bread. Write the letters of the alphabet, lower case and/or capital, on the bread shapes. Cut them apart. Have children put them in the correct order. The cards can be laminated and put in a center, or you can reproduce a copy for each child. Have them cut the loaves apart and paste them in order on a strip of butcher or construction paper.

2. Reproduce a copy of pages 40 and 41. Write a word on each loaf. The words you use will depend on the level of your students. Reproduce a copy for each child. Have them cut the loaves out and paste them in order to a sheet of paper.

first letter	second letter	third letter
bread	bagel	chapatis
cracker	biscuit	croissant
naan	cornbread	crumpet
pita	crumpet	wheat
rye	pita	white
tortilla	pumpernickel	

Handwriting

Use the words children are learning in this unit to practice manuscript or cursive writing. Write the words on the chalkboard and have children copy the list. Or write the words on a sheet of writing paper to be traced, then copied.

Listen for Parts of Words - Syllables

Say each word, have children listen for the separate parts they hear in each word, then say the word themselves, clapping out the number of syllables they hear.

one part - white, wheat, rye, French, naan
two parts - challah, cornbread, pita, croissant, biscuit, crumpet, bagel
three parts - chapatis, caraway, tortilla, inferra
four parts - pumpernickel

Writing Activities

Write a Description

Have children write a description of one of their favorite forms of bread. Have them include:

- how it looks
- how it tastes
- how you eat it

Make a Cookbook

You can find recipes for many types of ethnic breads in any good cookbook; however, the best recipes to include are those sent to class by the parents of your students. This becomes a great opportunity for children to share something of their culture as everyone learns how to make tortillas, chappatis, spoon bread, cornbread, etc. The contents will be a reflection of the diversity in your classroom.

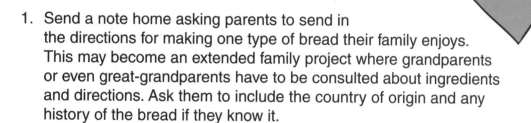

1. Send a note home asking parents to send in the directions for making one type of bread their family enjoys. This may become an extended family project where grandparents or even great-grandparents have to be consulted about ingredients and directions. Ask them to include the country of origin and any history of the bread if they know it.

2. Make a copy of each recipe for each child in class.

3. Have children make covers for the cookbooks from construction paper. Punch holes through the covers and pages and have children lace the pages.

Write a Story

Give your students some "starters" to choose from. Some students will use these, others will be eager to use a topic of their own. The only rule is that it relate to bread in some way.

Toast	The Day I Burned the Toast
Matzo Balls	If There was No Bread in the World
Pickle Sandwiches	Magic Muffins
Pizza Pie	How to Bake Bread

Write a Report

If your students are ready to do some research and writing on their own, have them select a kind of bread, go to the library to find out where it is from and how it is used, and write a one- or two-paragraph-report about what they learn.

Bread Shape Patterns

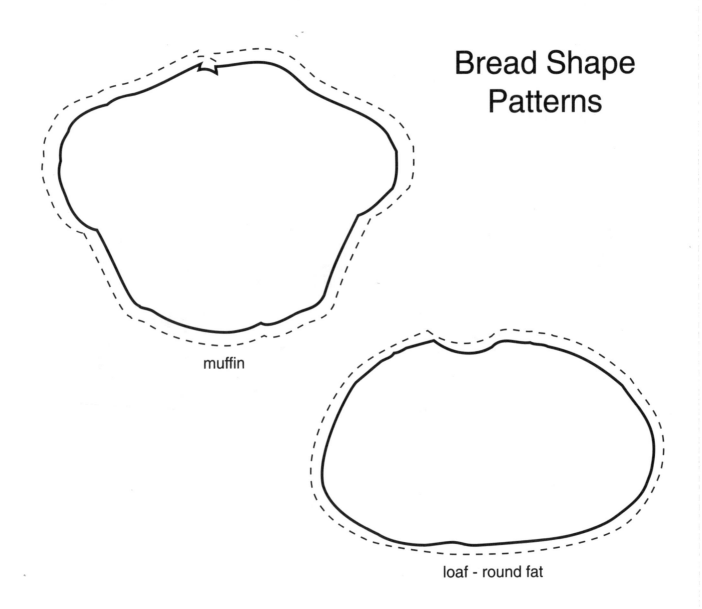

muffin

loaf - round fat

loaf - regular shape

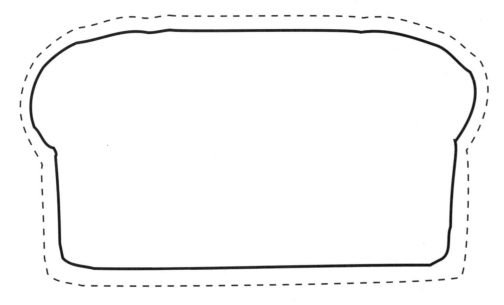

Bread Around the World

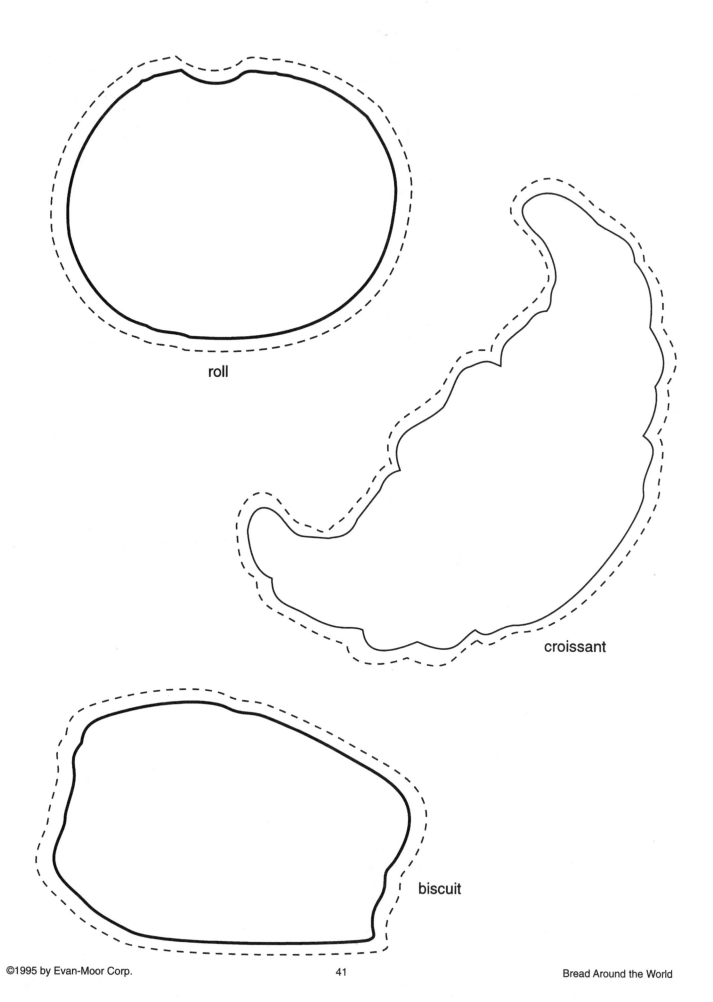

roll

croissant

biscuit

Bread Around the World

Rhymes and Chants

Warm toast,
Buttery toast,
Toast with jam,
In the morning.

Warm toast,
Buttery toast,
Toast with cheese,
At lunch time.

Warm toast,
Buttery toast,
Toast with stories
At bedtime.

Crumpling crackers.
Crumpling them up.
Crumpling crackers
Into my soup cup.

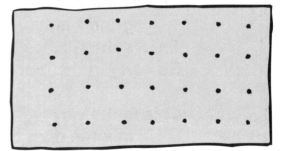

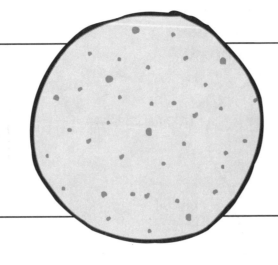

Tortilla and beans,
Tortilla and cheese,
Tortilla at snack time,
Just say "Please."

Bread Around the World

Sow the Seed

This is the way we sow the seeds,
   sow the seeds, sow the seeds.
This is the way we sow the seeds
So early in the morning.

This is the way we harvest the wheat,
   harvest the wheat, harvest the wheat.
This is the way we harvest the wheat
So early in the morning.

This is the way we grind the flour,
   grind the flour, grind the flour.
This is the way we grind the flour
So early in the morning.

This is the way we mix the dough,
   mix the dough, mix the dough.
This is the way we mix the dough
So early in the morning.

This is the way we eat the bread,
   eat the bread, eat the bread.
This is the way we eat the bread
So early in the morning.

Traditional Song

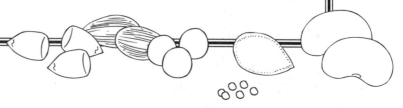

Lunch Time

Mom asked, "Do you want a sandwich for lunch?"
I answered, "Mom, I'd like that a bunch."

Mom asked, "What kind of sandwich will it be?"
I answered, "One of these is just right for me."

  pumpernickel and a bit of ham
  white bread and strawberry jam

  pita filled with pickled pigs knees
  bagel and lox and lots of cream cheese

  biscuits with butter and scrambled egg
  rye bread with slices of chicken leg

(Have your students make up more sandwiches of their own.
Real or "silly" are both fine.)

Muffin Man

Oh, do you know the muffin man,
    the muffin man, the muffin man,
Oh, do you know the muffin man
    who lives in Drury Lane?

Yes, we know the muffin man,
    the muffin man, the muffin man,
Yes, we know the muffin man,
    who lives in Drury Lane.

(Have your students make up variations using breads and
streets having more meaning to their lives. "Do you know
the bagel man who lives on Lighthouse Street?" "Do you
know the tortilla man who lives on Alvarado Drive?"

Bread Search

How many times can you find the word *bread*?

b	r	e	a	d	l	o	a	f	r	o	l	l
r	y	e	b	r	e	a	d	b	a	g	e	l
c	r	a	c	k	e	r	x	b	r	e	a	d
p	u	m	p	e	r	n	i	c	k	e	l	y
b	r	e	a	d	t	o	r	t	i	l	l	a
n	a	a	n	b	r	e	a	d	p	i	t	a
m	a	t	z	o	b	r	e	a	d	b	u	n

Challenge - Can you find these words about bread?

bagel	matzo	roll
bun	naan	rye
cracker	pita	tortilla
loaf	pumpernickel	

Bread Around the World

Write and Draw

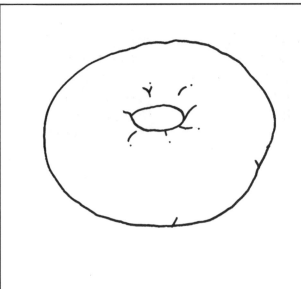

This is a _____

I like it with _____

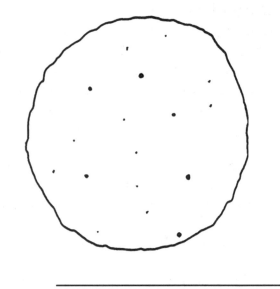

This is a _____

I like it with _____

This is a slice of _____

I like it with _____

This is _____ bread.

I like it with _____

Art Activities

Bread Collage

Collect as many magazines as you can find that have good pictures of foods, especially types of bread. Women's magazines and cooking magazines are good places to look. The "home" or "living" sections of newspapers sometimes have recipes with clear pictures. If you can accumulate enough appropriate magazines, have each child make his/her own collage. If not, divide children into small groups to make a cooperative collage on larger paper.

Materials:
- construction paper (for individual project)
- butcher paper (for group project)
- glue
- magazines, newspapers, etc.

Directions:
1. Have your students collect more than enough pictures to cover their paper. Have them trim or tear the pictures into various sizes.

2. Explain that they are to arrange the pictures on their paper until they have an arrangement they like. Pictures should overlap.

3. Have them spread a thin layer of glue along the edges of each picture (gluing only one at a time), laying it down, and rubbing it gently to be sure it sticks.

4. Let the collages dry, then have children trim any pieces of pictures that might be hanging over the edges of the paper.

5. Display the colorful collages around the classroom for everyone to enjoy.

Bakery Window

Have children paint delicious looking loaves of bread, stacks of rolls, and mountains of muffins in baskets and on plates and trays. Use these paintings to create a bulletin board of the front window of a bakery.

Materials:

for paintings:
- paint paper
- tempera
- brushes

for "bakery window"
- butcher paper - blue and brown
- construction paper - any color
- wide-tipped marking pens

Steps:

1. Have children paint their pictures. Set these aside to dry. When they are dry, have each child cut out his/her own painting.

2. Create a "bakery window" by covering a bulletin board with blue butcher paper. Create the window over this background using strips of brown butcher paper to make the window frame.

3. Cut the name of the "bakery" from construction paper and pin to the "window."

4. Place the children's paintings in the "window." Add price tags if you wish.